THE STATIC CLING PRINCIPLE

What You Attach to Your Life Alters Your Future

PAUL D. CASEY

Printed in the United States of America

First Printing, 2014

ISBN 978-0-9837874-2-6

Lightning Source Inc.

1246 Heil Quaker Blvd.

La Vergne, TN USA 37086

https://www1.lightningsource.com

Cover design by Laura Dyan Casey

Edited by Heather Villa

CONTENTS

FORWARD

As I have traveled through my life, two things have really surprised me:

1. ***What I am capable of; and***

2. ***Where I can find the positive influences that I want to stick in my life.***

I have been shocked to see what God can do through an ordinary guy like me. For me, a young man almost completely void of self-confidence, it was a matter of realizing what I wanted or wanted to do/accomplish, and then stepping out and taking the risk(s) necessary to reach the goal, while communicating with God, the Author and

Finisher of my faith and my life, on a regular basis, as to His associated intentions. In doing so, I have realized I can accomplish absolutely anything that is in line with His will, as I allow Him and His supernatural power to work in and through my life. Second, I have been surprised at the places, people and organizations that have most positively influenced my life, built my self-confidence and encouraged me to attempt to do great things. I would encourage you to be open to new ideas and willing to see possibilities in places where others might not be open.

Finally, I have realized, God has a plan for each and every one of our lives. A great plan! With that plan comes timing. So, just like the timing and tempo of a great song, I have learned that I need to walk in tune and in time with Him, and that experience is so much more pleasant than to be outside of His will.

This book will help give you guiding principles to find God's will for your life, do great things and "cast off everything that hinders or easily entangles us, and run with perseverance the race marked out before us." Hebrews 12:1 (paraphrased)

You can do great things! God has a great plan for your life! God and I believe in you and your potential! Read on!

--LTC, Deputy,

U.S. Representative Brad Klippert

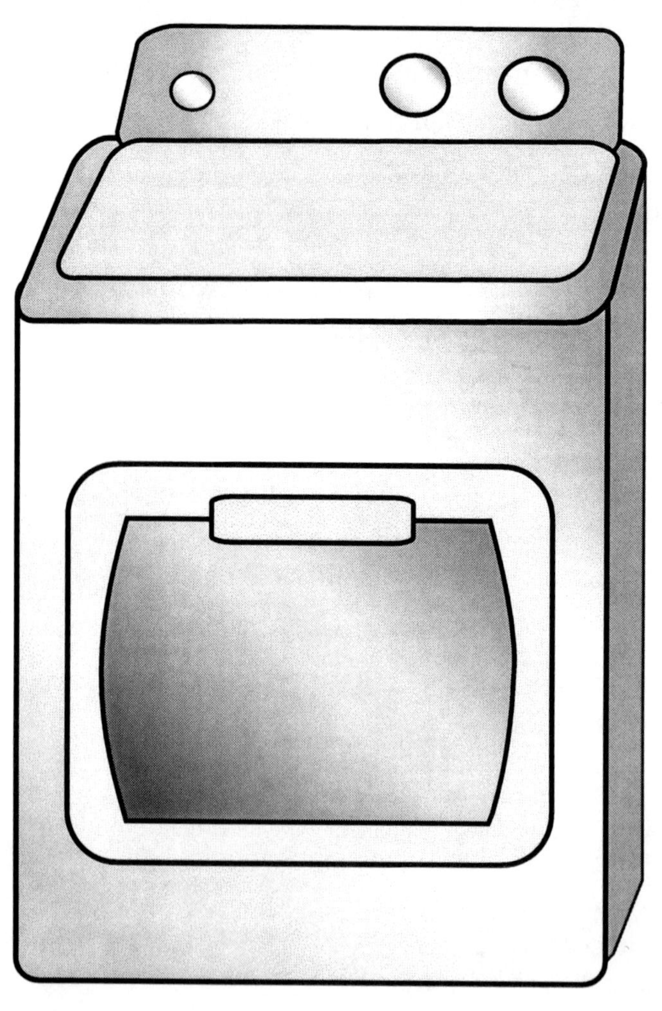

INTRODUCTION

So, I was taking the laundry out of the dryer, putting it in the basket, and trucking it upstairs for folding and putting away. You know the drill. A couple years spent as a single parent makes one more domestic, and there are chores that just need to get done. But there are more important priorities; so I try to tackle my chores as quickly as possible.

I'm whipping clothes into drawers and onto hangars, and then there's that annoying moment when static cling keeps a couple items together. Yes, it's a first-world problem, but it slows me down momentarily—and it gives me a big shock of static electricity the faster I try to separate the clothes.

For some reason, this time, it made me think. Probably because every life happening is a potential illustration to a public speaker.

First I thought to myself: *This is where all those socks go that seem to disappear in the dryer*. And then I thought: *These two items would probably stick to each other forever if they never were pulled apart. They would almost become one. The static electricity that keeps them together is quite powerful, almost irresistible to these light objects.*

What causes static cling? I heard it's called the triboelectric effect (thanks, Wikipedia). Low humidity allows static electricity to build up when two substances with opposite charges rub together (one positive, one negative). The perfect little storm for clinging. Conditions need to be just right for the sparks to fly or the attraction to stick. The dryness causes electrons to travel from one material to another. And that reminded me of when I was a kid and my dad rubbed a balloon on my head.

I reduce the clothes-clinging-together problem when I use fabric softeners and dryer sheets. But now I have these little Kleenex-type things lying around to pick up—not sure if I won that battle in the long run.

But, seriously, it made me realize how each one of us has our own kind of static cling working for or against us in our daily living. Life circumstances toss us about, like the dryer, and negativity seeks to adhere to our normally positive way of thinking. If we let it stick, it forms an unhealthy groove in our brain that we fall back into when under stress. We react the same way, we exhibit dysfunctional behavior, and we regret it later. It slows us down in pursuing the goals that we say mean the most to us. But it's our comfort zone, and we coddle our dysfunction, rationalizing its root cause away, saying, "Well, that's just the way I am."

Once in a while, someone confronts us on our issue or we hurt enough to want to change it, and we dig deep and give a new way of thinking and behaving a try. But we get shocked when we try to remove it. We experience discomfort. It's not a feeling we want to repeat. It seems easier to accept the discomfort than it is to deal with it. Because doing something is time-consuming. Doing nothing can cause another spark. Let's just leave that alone. Habits, unhealthy relationships, or mindsets stick to us another day, month, year, or longer.

Occasionally, we commit to removing what has clung to us for way too long, and we get help since we cannot do it alone. We find an antistatic person like a coach or counselor or mentor to give us some tools to pry that stinkin' habit off us. It forces us to carve out the time and the cash to deal with our issue, but we begin to break free—and it feels good to shed the boat anchor to a flourishing life.

How easy it is to live in default mode. Where we indiscriminately allow people and habits to attach to our lives, and then wake up at point Z languishing, wondering how we got messed up and defeated. We look to blame those people or the dark world around us, but if we are honest, we realize that we are the gatekeepers of our lives. We control what comes in and attaches to us, and what leaves us and attaches to others. Martin Luther once said: "You can't stop birds from landing on your head, but you can stop them from building a nest in your hair." Even though static cling is a powerful phenomenon, we have the power to build better defenses against it.

Life is more than playing defense. We need to carry the ball, connect with others, and grow from experiences. We need to generate our own electricity for getting these desires to stick and to shape our character, virtue, and influence.

That's what this book is about:
doing a self-evaluation to determine what you have allowed to adhere to your life and if it matches your values; what do you want to do about it; and in going forward, what do you intentionally want to stick more to your life. The buzzer just went off! Let's start by taking a look inside your life-dryer...

CHAPTER 1

How Do I Know it's Sticking to Me?

One of the most memorable scenes from the movie *The Incredibles* is when the superhero, muscular Mr. Incredible, tries to run from the evil Syndrome character who is trying to trap him. As he runs down the tunnel, Syndrome shoots black gobs at him. Mr. Incredible tries to fight them off. When the gobs make contact and stick to him, they begin to inflate like big balloons of silly putty that deny his forward progress and eventually suffocate him, temporarily rendering him unconscious.

That's one of the telltale signs of something that sticks to you in a negative sense. You try to fight it off, but succumb to the power you have given it over you. You go to it as a substitute for your life purpose. It has become your "shadow mission." Thus, your growth is stunted. It's like you have chewing gum on the bottom of your shoes. You stay right where you are and don't move forward, which, to be honest, means that you have begun to decline. Because I know that you only coast one direction—downhill.

How about a positive example of stickiness? I was in hurry to get my sophomore son home to bed following Boy Scouts because he had a zero-hour class (which is before I even wake up!). But we needed some groceries. I zipped us over to the store, and we drove past some homeless folks with signs asking for anything that could help them survive. Ignoring them, I found a parking spot near the front. Before I had turned off the engine, my son had cleaned out the change-holder from the front seat and told me, "I'll meet you inside, Dad." He proceeded to run across the parking lot to give the needy folks our loose change. I was never more proud.

Our church (and hopefully our parenting) had been modeling to have an others-focused life that pleases God who commanded us to love our neighbor as ourselves. My son had incorporated that value into his own life to the point of seeing a need, registering that he could do something about it, and springing into action. He didn't care that it was across the parking lot or that dad was in a hurry. The virtue stuck to him.

Positive or negative, something has static-like qualities in our life when:

- ***You let it stay.*** No decision is in itself a decision, and what we tolerate, we validate. If some stimulus comes toward you and you don't start barring the door of your heart to it, you have taken the first step toward passively letting it stick to you. That still isn't a deal-killer or a vow because static cling doesn't often happen after one pass. Remember, it takes regular friction to stick. It gets more powerful in your life when you continually allow it past your defenses, and say that's it OK for your life. You allow it/him/her to recline on your life-couch, and you offer it a drink and some food, saying "make yourself right at home and you can come back anytime." Then that behavior begins to form your character, which all habits do, or a person begins to influence your character, which all friends do.

- ***You put it regularly in front of you.*** Whether you pick up your phone, open up another pack, surf to that web site, or write it on your calendar, you know static cling is happening in your life when you begin taking actions that fill your life with more of it. It's like you are hanging a poster of it in your brain, saying this is what I aspire towards. You are symbolically clearing your counters to make space for this craving to have a prominent place in your life. You only have so much discretionary time. With what are you choosing to fill those moments outside of sleep and work? That answer shows you what is inching toward first place in your affections.

- ***It is impacting your day-to-day decisions.*** No matter what conversation you are in, you find yourself viewing it through the lens of this passion. You speak up to defend it, or build walls to protect its existence in your life. You work your life around it instead of vice-versa. It propels you forward until you can get more of it. Others begin to mirror back to you what they see happening in you because of it. Previous priorities get thrown to the back-burner.

- ***It becomes your default mode of living.*** At this stage, your autopilot response to anything in life is tinged with what has stuck to you. You cannot help it because it has become a part of you and will take a lot of difficult effort to remove it. It now drives you instead of you directing your life down other paths. You get defensive when anyone comes near it or speaks against it because it's like you are defending your family—this passion has become so dear to you. Take it away for a time period, and it's like going into withdrawals to exist without it.

"That which we love we grow to resemble." —St. Bernard of Clairvoux

Two other insights here: *The more emotional the tie to that habit or person, the more likely it sticks*. It's easy to shed what we aren't attached to emotionally. Whatever. Done. But lace it with heart-attachments, with something or someone you have really grown to care about deeply, and all deals are off. This will require surgery to extract, and a recovery period to grieve.

And just like meat in a marinade, *the longer you stay exposed to and accepting of this stimulus in your life, the more you will take on its scent and flavor*. That could be sweet-smelling if it's a positive influence, and quite rotten if it's a negative one. This is actually a strategy of brainwashing in prison camps, and also what the advertising profession hopes to subliminally influence your purchases. Layers of static cling are harder to peel off.

Let's head to the next chapter to start with forming positive attachments...

CHAPTER 2

Static Cling Working for You

I was with my kids at the Pacific Science Center in Seattle this past summer. Outside of the center are some fun hands-on activities, and one of them is this massive water cannon that you can aim at targets. Once the stream of water hits the target, it begins to spin radically, which looked pretty cool.

Similarly, you, and only you, control your life trajectory. Do you believe that? If so, then you are empowered to fill your life with positive adherences. Life offers many deeply-fulfilling opportunities, and it's your job to attach to them intentionally.

The late author, entrepreneur, and motivational speaker, Jim Rohn believed that life is not the filling of time but the collection of experiences—and the intensity and frequency of that collecting is up to you.

Virtues and strategic alliances with key people make a difference, causing a life rewarding cling. Sorry, no osmosis here--you have to get yourself ready to receive them.

Some of the themes for getting to the good stuff are:

- ***Self-discipline.*** In a previous life I was an elementary school principal, and I always thought it was good when students were caught for misbehavior—and I told them. When they looked at me like I was insensitive,

I explained in kid-terms that the purpose of school discipline was to help form self-discipline in them in the long run.

You cannot depend on external motivators to push yourself to greatness in life. It comes down to making the right choices every day, even if means denying yourself the easy routes that lead away from success.

"Success seems to be largely a matter of hanging on after others have let go." – William Feather

It's like you keep licking the envelope until it stays sealed.

- ***Delayed gratification.*** Someone once said, "You never saw a fish on the wall with its mouth shut." One of my kids is a saver and one is a spender (I will protect the innocent by not telling you which is which.). The spender has the dickens of a time letting the dollars not burn a hole in his/her pocket. We are working on the pause before the purchase. In a world where we can get anything at our fingertips almost instantly, you apply the self-discipline by not impulsively grabbing whatever/whoever is within your reach—if it's not healthy for your progress. You are delaying gratification of what is second best in order to pursue what is actually best and in line with your values and life vision. Like a suitcase with too many labels on it, when you want to stick something on it that is really cool, you are out of room because you stuck too many less-important labels on it to fill it up.

- ***An appropriate worldview.*** Personally, I am a man of faith and have chosen a Bible-based worldview of life. A worldview is the lens with which you see everything around you. Everyone has to choose a worldview, and it's through those glasses that you interpret your circumstances—choose carefully if you want static cling working in your favor. Everything you do starts with a thought, then is screened by your worldview, then turns into an action. To begin to identify yours, circle and then rank your most important values in the appendix of this book. Your values are your DNA, and all your decisions in life (dealing with time, relationships, purchases, etc.) should line up with them in order to live a life in alignment. You know what happens when your tires get out of alignment, right?

- ***Outward focus.*** Say it aloud, "It's not about me!" Did you choke on the words? Two things I know: You are not the center of the universe. And, you were not wired for isolation. Even if you are an introvert (getting filled up by time alone), you are a relational being--and it's only when you get myopic ("all I see is me") that you decline to narcissistic tendencies and allow destructive static cling. Ingrown toenails are painful!

Treating others as they want to be treated is golden for many reasons. Holding others in high regard impacts the decisions you make, and usually (unless co-dependent) leads to better outcomes for you and them. You cannot illuminate another's path without also lighting your own. And, the best way to forget your own problems is to help someone solve theirs. My experience has been that I've turned the corner in recovery from a trauma when I begin to serve those around me instead of remaining in my self-centered mud-puddle.

- ***Passion.*** Now again, passion can go both ways, but your life can never take off without it. It's the motor in your engine. It's your drive to succeed and flourish. I had a boss correct me when I was over-eager on an assignment, and when he asked what I learned; I told him I should probably dial-down my passion. He said, "You can make other changes, but never dial-down your passion." A rolling stone gathers no moss, or said another way: a person living with passion for the right things does not collect layers of negative attachments.

No one wants to associate with a stick in the mud; it's just not attractive. Evaluate what you stand for, what your heart breaks for, what you'd die for—and you will have a wound-up engine that is primed for the right kind of attachments. It will also be the impetus toward getting started on your quest, since passion for something is the best way to beat procrastination.

Self-analysis process tool for the positives

- ❏ Do I possess the self-discipline to stick to the right priorities?
- ❏ Can I pause and filter opportunities without impulsively grabbing at all of them?
- ❏ Have I nailed down my values and worldview to orient a proper perspective?
- ❏ Do I balance an emphasis on others with taking care of myself?
- ❏ Am I lit up with enough passion to keep momentum moving forward?

Every choice you make consistently has a payoff, or you would stop choosing it. You make a to-do list so that you can check it off. You hang out with that guy because he compliments you every time you are together and thus feeds your self-worth. You donate your excess clothes because of the good feeling you get for being philanthropic and/or living with more simplicity and less clutter. Since every choice has consequences, here are some positive payoffs for making static cling work for you and your future success:

- ***Good results.*** When you plant good seeds and nurture them, you get good fruit. When you commit to a diet, you start seeing results that keep you motivated. Supervisors at work are primarily concerned with results, when it comes right down to it, and employees have been given lots of flexibility if they will keep producing. Keeps the momentum going when you are adhering things and people to your life that get you closer to your goals and life-vision. And I would recommend journaling your results as markers along the way to success.

- ***An anchored life.*** I use the word *anchor* here in a good, grounding-yourself way, not a holding-back way. If you find a good fishing spot, you want to drop anchor and hover in that area to reel in even more. I have been through California earthquakes and can attest that no one wants to constantly experience a shifting foundation under them. It's unsettling, to say the least!

  Positive stuff that sticks again and again gives you more self-confidence and also causes you to be more resilient (quick bounce-backs) when difficulties hit your life. You are not swayed back to allowing the negative to stick to you because your internal compass keeps you on the right path, pointed toward your "true north."

- ***Trustworthiness.*** No one wants to depend on someone who waffles in their life or decisions. I think that's what makes me most irritated when it comes to political campaigns.

One of the best compliments you can get is that you are grounded (not like a teenager, though), or firm in your footing. With the right kinds of things sticking to you, you become true to yourself and make consistent choices that people around you at work and home can count on. You will come through. Trust begets more trust, and relationships continue to get stronger.

- ***Impact beyond self.*** I think that deep-down, we all want to make a difference in this life we live. We are not simply taking up space on this planet, but there is a great need in the world with which our talents and passion must intersect and address. Whenever I volunteer for a community organization, I feel like I am joining with like-minded people who care, in order to lighten a heavy load. Getting healthier as a person gives you the strength to reach out beyond your own life-dramas to relieve the stress on those less fortunate, who are counting on someone to help them get them through a season. Wouldn't it be great if they could draw upon your strength without sucking all the life out of you?

Speaking of sucking the life out of you, let's address that pain in chapter 3....

CHAPTER 3

Static Cling Working Against You

The wisest man who ever lived was named Solomon, and he was the third king of ancient Israel. Although he had great wisdom at the beginning of his term of office, he surely didn't show it in the end. When he was following his God for wisdom, he succeeded and was the talk of the known world. When he decided to hoard horses and marry hundreds of women from all religious backgrounds, contrary to his values, his downfall began—and he didn't finish strong.

Negative adherences will take you down, usually over time, gradually eroding your values until you are not the person you want to be and become. Your friends or family members might even say, "This isn't the person I know!" It's insidious because of how subtle the temptations often cause us to act in ways we normally wouldn't act. At first, it doesn't seem to be a big deal. It isn't hurting anyone—except you. You can handle it, right? You try to slide your dirt under your life's rug, but it becomes a tripping hazard. The broken-record pain of clinging to this hurtful thing is slowly destroying the vibrancy of your life.

Let's put this all into context. Categories to <u>be on the lookout for in your life include</u>:

- ***Addictions.*** These are substances or habits that have power over your choices. They can be hard addictions (like illegal drugs or pornography) or soft addictions (like too many hours of TV or gallons of ice cream). You believe you cannot live without them. Their draw is strong and can take over your time and money decisions. You unknowingly have begun to worship them. Temporarily, they give a "high" feeling, but usually a "low" comes in between "fixes", and a feeling of regret accompanies this downer. If you are willing to lie or steal or betray or secretly hide for the opportunity to have or protect having this thing, you are most likely addicted to it.

- ***Hypocrisy.*** I remember the character Two-Face in one of the Batman movies, and you never knew which side of him you were going to experience. Those lacking integrity hold people hostage by saying one thing and doing another, or flip-flopping a decision they have made for a better offer or to be a pleaser. By not being grounded, you just get blown around by the wind of opinions and moods, and no one can get close to you nor trust you.

- ***Destructive inputs.*** Garbage in, garbage out. If you are regularly attaching yourself to movies, TV, web sites/blogs, music lyrics, books/magazines, or acquaintances that run contrary to your values or the life you've always wanted; these will take your life in the opposite direction, one negative thought at a time. You tolerate it even though it internally makes you wince. You might say it doesn't affect you,... doesn't affect you, doesn't affect you. If you think of it being just a little poop baked into your brownie, would you still eat it? Growing up, I was taught that you become like the things you read and the people you associate with, some of whom could be...

- ***Manipulative people.*** Guilt trips, flattery, yanking your chain--manipulators are only out to use you for their pleasure, to get their needs met by sucking the life out of you. They try to convince you that you want what they want, and without a strong enough backbone, you cave to their wiles. They may say that their motives are pure, but how much value are they adding to the relationship? They use the word love, but are they showing that love is an action not a feeling? It is critical to evaluate your relationships to beware of someone that may be dragging you down to their selfish level.

Self-analysis process tool for the negatives

- ❑ Do I have a hard/soft addiction that I just cannot live without?

- ❑ Do I frequently bail on commitments or change my mind and let people down?

- ❑ Am I watching or listening to media that runs contrary to my values?

- ❑ Am I in relationship with someone who is using me for his/her own advantage?

Of course, there are payoffs to continuing to attach to these maladies, but none of them are healthy. We can rationalize anything, right? It usually takes brutal honesty with yourself or from those closest to you, in order to see the dysfunction in yourself. Why is that? The dysfunction has become the new normal, and has started to become part of your identity, whether you feel the pain yet or not.

Let me put out a warning to you here: these are the <u>negative consequences that accompany static cling that you don't pull off:</u>

- *Getting and staying stuck.* When you are carrying excess baggage, it gets difficult to keep moving in the right direction. It's like lining up for a race after eating at a buffet. I'm content right here, thank you very much. After a while it's too hard to get around and there is no traction toward your life purpose and priorities. Newton said objects at rest tend to stay at rest. Have you ever not gone to the gym or church or your parents' house, and each day it gets harder to get in the car and go there?

Stuck is a depressing place to hang out, but most people are stuck in at least one area of their lives.

- ***No impact.*** The more negative stuff clinging to you, the more you have to maintain it. Naturally, you turn inward and less outward. I call this "going dark" like in the spy movies when the hero goes "off-comm" so that he/she cannot be heard anymore. When those in my life have gone dark, I know they are making poor choices and don't want to be exposed or confronted on them. It's at this time that your influence on others becomes minimal. Sometimes, you might even be embarrassed to be with others; and you pull in even more. People come looking for you in your cave for a while, and then leave you alone.

- ***Treadmill living.*** On a treadmill, you expend energy but don't actually go anywhere. At least at the gym you are burning calories. But in life, if you are busy, but not doing the right things, it feels like you are chasing your tail (something I tease my wife about when she misplaces something she needs to move on with her day). You get to the end of the day and wondered if you accomplished anything at all of importance—because you were consumed with the cling-ons. It's just surviving, not thriving. It's like that movie *The Truman Show*, where the main character goes through the motions each day without realizing there is more out there. Very short-sighted and not long-term—living for the now at the expense of the future.

- ***Distracted.*** My dad used to say about one of his easily-distracted volleyball players, "She is other-directed", and he meant what we now call ADD-like symptoms of not staying on track. ADD is a real condition, but someone with negative adherences can't focus their energies completely in a positive direction. They are on rabbit trails, often filled with drama, that don't lead to productivity or deeper relationships.

They break promises and don't follow-through. They have the "squirrel" mentality of loving the next new thing that comes across their radar and don't want to do the hard internal work of shedding the lint.

- ***Believing lies.*** Yes, we all have voices in our heads. The key to life is deciding which voice to listen to. The saboteur voice finds ways to shoot yourself in the foot with its lies ("You'll never get that job interview if you try" or "Just stay here on the couch and eat some more chocolate"). The rationalizer voice tells you it's OK to cling to dysfunction ("It's not hurting anyone" or "She didn't mean that verbal abuse"). The procrastinator voice tells you to start dealing with it tomorrow, but for today it's just fine to stay where you are. Heeding those voices and their lies makes you start believing your own press releases, which keeps you standing still and stopping success.

With all that baggage, people around you wonder why you seem to be blind to your illness. Your family schedules an intervention with you or your boss puts you on a performance improvement plan, and you are surprised! Self-awareness is the ability to look at yourself honestly for both your strengths and weaknesses, and to clearly see the impact your behavior has on others. This key trait gets worn down to nothing when the static electricity of life builds up and you have no method of self-assessment nor feedback from caring others. Then that's when everyone else can see what's happening to you except you.

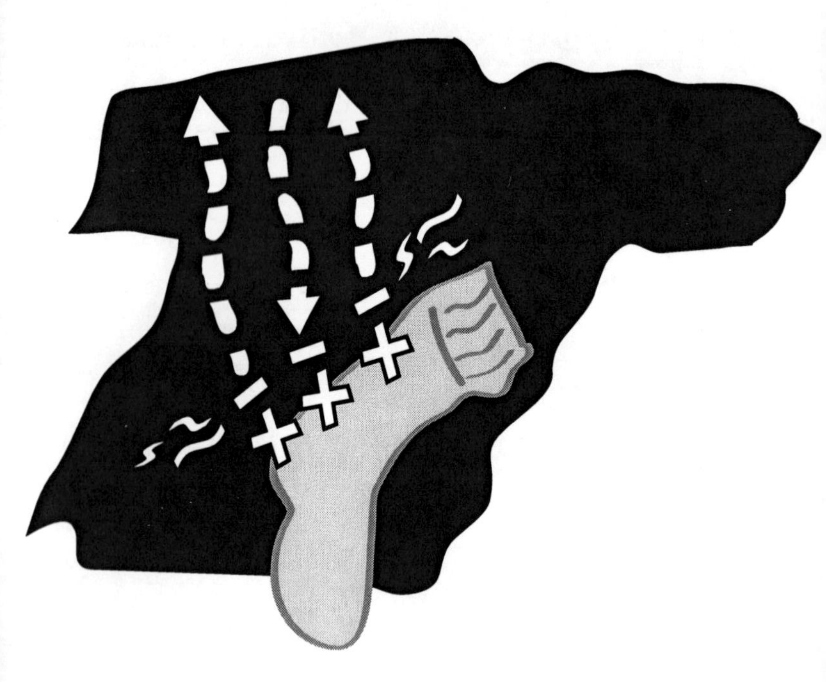

CHAPTER 4

How Do You Intentionally Stick the Right Things to Your Life?

Many people drift through their lives, being carried along by the waves of busyness, but not actually heading anywhere specifically. I was having dinner at my wife's work party years ago, and struck up a conversation with the twenty-something guy next to me, who was sitting by his girlfriend. I customarily ask questions to get people talking about themselves, looking for something common connection . I asked him about his job. He had none. I asked about his hobbies. He had none. I asked about his dreams. He had none. I wondered what attracted his girlfriend to him, but I didn't say that. The young adult had nothing going for him, and it made me want to scream, "Get a coach!" Get some help in discovering the life you could have!

Granted, because of your schedule, it is difficult to sit down in solitude and set some goals that will get you to a vision of making a difference in this life. Intentionality takes carved-out planning time. I take one hour a month minimum to assess my goals to determine my path, and then time each week to look at those goals to turn them into action plans. Very few people I've met get goals down on paper. They live on "Someday Isle," as motivational speaker Brian Tracy says. "Someday, I'll get to my bucket list. Someday, I'll work on my relationship. Someday, I'll start exercising. And someday never comes."

I heard the term "selective imbeddedness" the other day, and it means being careful and then confident in choosing what you want to go all-out pursuing. You probably have either been told by your supervisor or friend in a heart-to-heart talk about what behavior you need to change, or you have gotten yourself in hot water enough times and suffered enough consequences that some behavior has risen to the top of your list that must be implemented in order to grow forward.

"Growth Areas" Evaluation

- ❏ Marriage/relationship intimacy
- ❏ Choosing good friendships
- ❏ Eating habits/nutrition
- ❏ Fitness
- ❏ Leisure time spent
- ❏ Addiction to quit
- ❏ Professional growth
- ❏ Fear to conquer
- ❏ Productivity
- ❏ Forgiveness of the past
- ❏ Personal leadership
- ❏ Appropriate boundaries
- ❏ Continuing education
- ❏ Faith connection

When you have the priority growth item nailed down, here are <u>three super-glue steps to attaching what you want out of life to your life:</u>

1. ***Believe it.*** Your strategy can never be better than the understanding of your situation. Once you decide the habit or type of person you want to build more into your life, convince yourself of the benefits of staying the course, and that you have or will have what it takes to surround yourself with more of it. This voice of abundance is the voice in your head to listen to, but it must shout louder than the negative (scarcity) ones who are constantly making excuses. Take this new commitment seriously. Put it in writing and speak it aloud in the presence of others. After you are "all in", you...

2. ***Feed it.*** What you feed, grows. A Native American story illustrates this: A grandson told of his anger at a schoolmate who had done him an injustice. Grandfather said: "Let

me tell you a story. I, too, have felt a great hate for those that have taken so much, with no sorrow for what they do. But, hate wears you down and does not hurt your enemy. It is as if there are two wolves inside me: one is good and does no harm. He lives in harmony with all around him and does not take offense when no offense was intended. But the other wolf is full of anger. The littlest thing will set him into a fit of temper. It is hard to live with these two wolves inside me, for both of them try to dominate my spirit." The boy looked intently into his grandfather's eyes and asked, "Which one wins, Grandfather?" The grandfather solemnly replied, "The one I feed."

Speaking of feeding, don't bite off more than you can chew right away in your eagerness to make the static cling principle work for you. Discouragement is right around the corner ready to point out your failure and tell you to quit. Start small. Make doable goals. There are two common acronyms for clues to writing great goals. One is SMART: a goal must be specific (not general), measurable (you will know when it is achieved), attainable (it's doable), relevant-to-your-vision (not peripheral), and time-dated (has a deadline). The other is HARD: a goal must be heartfelt (you have an emotional connection to it), animated (you can visualize its accomplishment and how to get there), required (to get to the vision), difficult (it will stretch you to do it). Write a goal right now and see if it passes the test because if you can't visualize it, you can't do it.

Have you heard the saying that goals get their power when they cross the lips and pencil tips? Once the goal is written, display it in places you will often see it, because a goal not visible gets shuffled to the bottom of your paperwork piles and then forgotten. (Can you tell it's happened to me?) Put it on your mirror, your dashboard, or your computer monitor. Then share it with everyone to give it power:

your family, your friends, your colleagues, and your social media friends. Somewhere along the line one or more of them will ask you how it's going on your goal, and it will keep you accountable to staying on track. That's what I had to do with writing this book: I carved out the time and the location, wrote the outline in advance, and told my Facebook friends I was going to do it so that I'd keep pushing forward with the belief that I wanted to become a reality. Our lives tend to move in the direction we put our energy.

Another suggestion is to trigger the goal; in other words, what you will do to prepare to take the action. Taking a deep breath, saying personal affirmations, putting out your gym clothes—these are practical examples of triggers that launch your goal. Finally, since you become what you hang around, put yourself around people who are headed the same direction that you are. Join a club or support group, or start a success-partner group yourself with like-minded individuals that are FOR each other. I am in a Mastermind group where we set goals, and then we report our successes and our struggles a month later, submitting to coaching from each other to accelerating toward our goals.

3. ***Schedule it.*** Daily! Leadership guru and prolific author John C. Maxwell says the secret to success is what you do daily. I'm a little anal when it comes to time-management: scheduled to the fifteen-minute increment, color-coded by type of task, etc. I have never been able to make a to-do list and simply go down the list and check them off. Too easy to ignore. I have made a habit of making appointments with myself at work in order to get each of my to-do list items done. At home, I make an appointment with myself during a discretionary time period (evening or weekend blocks) to get a personal or business priority accomplished. It's the main

way I beat procrastination and keep juggling all that's on my plate.

Some say it takes twenty-one days of doing something new to make it into a habit, some say thirty, some say one hundred. Whatever the actual number, you have to do it daily to drive it into your value system and own it. If you miss a day, you get back on the horse and assure it gets plugged in tomorrow. Unsuccessful people give up instead of quickly going into problem-solving mode to figure out why this day was missed. "The person interested in success has to learn to view failure as a healthy, inevitable part of the process of getting to the top," counsels Dr. Joyce Brothers. You decide to fail forward, meaning that you use it as a learning experience. As long as you haven't given up, technically you haven't failed.

Bottom line--Random implementation never works! Your default comfort zone mode is

> too strong and will pull you back into old habits and patterns that took more than one hundred days to form. You are not going to assimilate it overnight. Just keep putting one step in front of the other every day in your chosen direction.
>
> In the confrontation between the stream and the rock, the stream always wins…not through strength, but through persistence.

And the behaviors you don't want? Starve them! If you don't the wolf inside you to grow up and take over, you must remove, cancel, and throw out the beast to pursue the new, healthier you. Christine Caine, musician and motivational author and speaker, says: "To keep moving forward you must learn to shake it off, let it go, drop it."

You want to be like Teflon
and steer clear of the shackles
of energy-sapping cling-ons?
Read on...

CHAPTER 5

How Do You Not Let Bad Stuff Stick to Your Life?

Defense is important: to our nation's security, on the football field, and even while driving. We all need a plan for antistatic defense so, like dandruff on a shirt, we don't have clingy stuff on us that keep us stagnant, beaten down, and maybe even embarrassed.

Let's start with the wrong way, which might be how you got here in the first place. I call it the

"Putting up a wall know-it-all." It's hard to speak into such a person. Their life is a fortress with guard dogs, gun turrets and barbed wire around. When you try to get in, alarms go off in their mood and it is clear that you have trespassed. You see, they already know everything: what is broken and what is just fine, what could be done to fix it and why they are delaying that process. Another simple word for this condition is pride.

Another way to crash and burn is to live a passive life, one in which you live out everyone else's script for your life except yours. Passive people let life just come to them, and they take it all in—the opposite of taking life by the tail and actively pursuing your greatest passions, strengths, and dreams. With unending tolerance, passive people never say No (because they haven't found their unique voice) and get taken advantage of easily, and later regretting that they were pushovers. Without emotional strength, static cling is almost automatic and then very difficult to remove later.

How does a person get on that wrong road?

- ***They stopped learning.*** I supervised some employees who were always looking to get out of professional development opportunities, and it saddened me. Somewhere along the way, they stopped reading books about getting to the next level, stopped being curious about a new way of living or new methods to try, stopped hanging around and networking with people who were growing and changing. They sat and stagnated like a backyard puddle. Lots of bacteria and mosquitoes like stagnating pools, but you don't see a lot of refreshment. Those just allowing static cling to happen have closed their minds and ears to sources of truth and health, stunting their growth. Their body is getting older, but their mind is frozen, years behind in maturity.

  Oftentimes these folks have created a very comfortable world where they are king/queen, and are in control of that world. A suggestion to change is met with resistance because it would rock that world off-kilter. They do not realize that in order to grow, there must be change—but it's just not that crucial to them.

- ***They didn't heed their warning gauges.*** We all have gauges unique to each of us that run hot as a warning signal that we are heading down unhealthy paths. Without taking note and making adjustments, their lives crash like a plane—but they could have gotten ahead of the mayday call by making an in-flight adjustment instead of staying on a doomed autopilot. For some, it's becoming more irritable; for others like me, it's a lack of creativity; others say they are more tired or have less capacity to handle all their roles. I've known people with anger issues that knew they were getting close to stepping over the line, but didn't get therapy for it—and they lost a job or a very dear relationship when one day they blew up and lost it all. Warning gauges are our friends; ignore them at your peril.

- ***They avoided intimacy with others.*** Married couples are supposed to be on an unending journey toward intimacy with each other—a deep knowing of one another that comes from transparency of feelings shared and greater trust and a desire to light up the other's biggest dreams. Those with layers of the heavy static cling have pulled out of this process. They guarded their conversations and protected their backsides. When someone got too close, they separated from them. No one really knows who they are at their core. It's almost like this person just goes through the motions like a robot without feelings. Self-protection doesn't have many good outcomes, except maybe on the Serengeti.

All of those above-traits are all conquerable. They are only dead-ends for as long as you allow them to be. "Realize that you cannot change until you accept you must change and decide to take charge of the rest of your life." –Paul/Sarah Edwards

On the flipside, there is a better way for keeping negative cling-ons at bay for the most part:

- ***A continuous improvement mentality.*** "An open mind collects more riches than an open purse." Many companies tout that they are a learning organization, and that is impressive. The StrengthsFinder assessment, an online leadership tool, revealed one of my top five strengths as "Maximizer." That means that whatever I touch or whatever I am a part of, I naturally try to make it better, to take it to the next level. Nothing is ever at its apex; there is always a new learning that can help turn a corner to greater success. Find a way to create a feedback loop from certain people who you know are for you, asking them to mirror back to you what they are seeing are your priorities these days, and what they are wondering about in your behavior. This takes great humility, but since the evaluation is coming from trusted advisors, you know they will say it in such a way as to promote your success, not crush your feelings.

Mentors who teach and coaches who process life with you should also be added to your support team in order to stay current and out of ruts. Ruts are graves with the ends kicked out! Toss in a counselor when you detect an emotional problem that needs solving and an accountability partner who relentlessly asks you if you've taken your next action—and you'll have "relational rebar" that will keep you standing when life-tornadoes hit you.

- ***Healthy disciplines.*** Disciplines may sound like a harsh word and one to avoid, especially if you have a history in the principal's office. But they are essential habits that center you on your priorities, and prevent rust from forming on your life. Your connection to God can be one of these, as I believe having a strong spiritual component in your life that holds each one of us together. It's the first thing I pursue after my shower every morning, and it starts my days with such peace that I cannot even explain.

Prayer and meditation and solitude are great disciplines for blocking out the constant noise of life and quieting your spirit to listen for what is out of whack and what needs to happen to re-orient. Nurturing friendships and therapeutic hobbies that encourage and refresh also guard against burnout, which lowers your resistance to static cling enemies. And finding a way to serve those in need in your neighborhood or community will also prevent a self-centered life-focus.

- ***An open heart for others.*** Yes, it is a risk to open yourself up to your family and friends and co-workers. Some people have been burned when they finally were authentic, as it was used against them in an argument—and that's just plain sad. But before you put the wall up and say "I'll never trust and be hurt again," I would encourage you that it is worth the risk. I would rather err on the side of deeper relationships than on the side of becoming more of a hermit any day! It is with people that life's greatest joys occur. As I mentioned earlier, we are wired to live in community with others. In that give-and-take relationship, both people's needs get met and life goes from gray to a vibrant color. And when you have healthy relationships, you repel the unhealthy people along with attitudes/habits that destroy that health in them.

Before we leave this chapter on keeping bad stuff from attaching to your life, I must add a section on setting appropriate boundaries, which are a fence and gate of protection around your life. Boundaries keep the good stuff at your core, released by you with others when you are strong—and keep any unhealthy invaders on the outside, not assimilated into your daily experience. Don't expect someone else to come to your rescue, especially if you got yourself into the mess by not putting up and sticking to your boundaries. You control the gate!

You will lose your stickiness on what is healthy within you if you let these invaders storm the gate past your boundaries:

- ***Drama.*** I liked that club in high school, but now it's a good thing to let the drama train roll right on by. Why? Because it's exhausting for people to dump their explosive issues at your doorstep and to expect you to jump into it with them. People that need lots of crises in their life are unstable, and you need some emotional distance from them to not wrap up in it. It's like a black hole that is very difficult to get out of, and you will be the one who gets hurt at the end when they are at their darkest hour.

- ***Financial bondage.*** P.T. Barnum said: "Money is in some respects like fire: it is a very excellent servant, but a terrible master." Going into debt puts undue stress on all your relationships. That bondage sits in the back of your mind like a tumor, always putting pressure on your thoughts and actions. Each creditor's bill is like a knife in your gut. So many arguments are birthed from money issues. Living paycheck to paycheck is also stressful because you are one month away from being broke, limiting your options.

- ***Vices that eat your lunch.*** Any of the seven deadly sins or their relatives that are clinging to you forms a barrier against the life you've always wanted. Not getting help for them makes it worse, for it seems that you have resigned to its control over your life and the collateral damage that it causes on those you love, who want you to break free. Don't even flirt with things that can pull the rug out from under you, for the gravitational pull will drag you down.

- ***Negativity.*** I have known people close to me that are like Eeyore on Winnie the Pooh: they are looking for the ax to fall, the other shoe to drop, and the thorn among the roses.

Hanging around these wet-blankets will start to seep that negativity into your speech. After a while, you will be catching yourself gossiping, condemning others, being holier than thou, cynical, and critical. Joy gets squished out, and it becomes hard to see the bright side of things. This frown-through-life mentality will cost you.

- ***Unforgiveness.*** Bitterness is like voluntarily putting on a set of handcuffs and going through life choosing to keep the shackles on. You are holding the grudge, and the other person is off skiing in Colorado. It's like an IV drip of poison that you plug in every morning that you choose not to forgive someone who has offended you. It becomes the elephant in the room, and others begin to have to look around the elephant to try to find the real you. Unforgiveness is a growth-stunter, for sure.

Hopefully, that convinced you to get your shields up, as they say in Star Trek.

Boundaries, or what you say No to, will allow you to say Yes to these bright outcomes:

- ***Traveling light.*** By not allowing the negative static cling, you don't have the baggage that many others have. And it feels more peaceful to not put that bulky backpack of issues on your back on your way to work each day. Then the Big Mo of momentum is on your side, as you commit to not bringing anything on your journey that will slow you down. It's like how it's easier to keep a house clean once it's clean.

- ***Others are influenced.*** If you have kids, they see a role model of good lifestyle choices. If you have co-workers and friends, they are drawn into what you have that they don't. People search you out for your recommendations on how they can have better boundaries because they see you unfettered by unwanted cling-ons. Bonus: you attract the right kind of comrades now that your "picker" is fixed.

- ***Seeing possibilities.*** Before, when you were in your sticky mess, everything looked dark and your options seemed limited. But now, it's like the horizon opened up. It's like eliminating a bunch of commitments on your calendar and feeling for the first time the space to relax and be present with people. You can now better screen the opportunities that inevitably come your way through the filter of your values because you are secure in who you are, what you stand for and where you are going. And even take wise risks without fear!

- ***Good health.*** Less stress leads to fewer junk food meals for comfort or from a crazy schedule. More time doing what you want to be doing, not what you have been guilted into doing, allows you to exercise as a priority. And it won't be long before you attract a workout buddy. Since most health problems are induced by stress, a cling-free life purges your system of those "dis-eases" brought on by weak boundaries.

And now, the moment

you've all been waiting for...

CHAPTER 6

How Do You Pull Off Unwanted Stuff that is Already Stuck on You?

You know what you want to stick to you. You know how to prevent negative static cling, and now you realize that there are a few areas that you must peel off your life to start these new habits. But we all know that the static electricity will give you a shock that may make you recoil from the courageous course of action. Some things fall off pretty easily; some are very hard to pry loose with a crowbar. I have coached a few people who made strides in the right direction, but when the going got rough, they digressed back to their old way of living. And they regretted it. Life is too short for regrets.

Let's be real. You have a part of your life that needs removal, and it's very possible that you will encounter these obstacles in the process:

- ***The quick give-up.*** If I asked you to cross your arms a different way than you are used to, it would feel awkward—and you'd quickly go back to the more comfortable way. Same with pulling off the sticky items: when sparks fly, the automatic response is to let the static cling items just stay where they are. Your resolve wasn't intense enough, and if it will cause more shocks, maybe it's just best to avoid that pain. You say, "It was a good idea, but..."

- ***Rationalization*** and his cousin denial will find some good reason to keep your life stuck right where it is. This happened just tonight when I made the poor choice at the restaurant during my quest to fast from junk food. "Maybe I am making too big a deal out of this," you say. "It's only one little issue. We can all have our one vice, right?" Your sympathetic friends will easily talk you out of it because they have gotten used to this version of you and want to keep you at their level. Isn't it interesting how people get threatened when someone around them decides to grow?

- ***Staying busy and running past it.*** You can run, but you can't hide. We can all blame our schedules, the fast pace of life for not doing hard internal work. It's almost like a badge of courage these days: being busy. It's like we are passing out our resume for living on this planet by all the running around we do. Well, you can only run so far before your cling-on catches up to you and you are forced to deal with it—and it's usually at the least opportune time.

- ***Getting too close to the bad influences again.*** My youth pastor growing up used to use the illustration of why would you walk on the edge of the pool if you couldn't swim. At any time, you could fall in and drown. Why not stay as far away as possible from tempting situations? Flirting with disaster may be a self-fulfilling prophecy that you don't really want to come true. Take the donuts off the counter if you want to avoid eating donuts.

But you are not going to go there, right? Wanting to change, but doing nothing to pull it off you, and then expecting different results is that always-present definition of... insanity. It's not going to magically go away without a crusade against it.

Like that little bottle of Goo-Be-Gone in the garage, take these cling-removal actions

and push through the shock and withdrawal to a new tomorrow:

- ***Associate with healthy people.*** Surround yourself with people that align with your values, who have habits that you admire, and who you will let speak into your life when they see you drifting. It's amazing that I order the healthy foods when someone at the restaurant with me makes a healthy choice, too! And when my friend comments that the person who is criticizing me is not good for me due to their unresolved wounds, I can more easily detach. Health attracts health, and it will make dysfunction stand out as undesirable.

- ***Let go—once and for all.*** John Maxwell says, "You give up to go up." You need to unclench your fist around your once-prized (but harmful) possession, and completely say No to its power over you. And it's OK to grieve the loss, because even though it's a good loss, it's still leaving a hole in your life. Recap its destructive power in your life and say good-bye. This frees you up to create a new future. Bernadette McAliskey says, "To gain that which is worth having, it may be necessary to lose everything else."

- ***Replace the bad with good habits.*** "Effort is only effort when it begins to hurt," philosophizes Jose' Ortega y Gasset. You can't just not do something. Make an action plan and start implementing it immediately to fill your life with the people, learnings, habits, and character traits that get you to your desired future, or else old habits will rush back into the void.

- ***Schedule regular check-ups with a coach, mentor, or success partner.*** These professionals want you to succeed, and are an objective, non-emotional source of support for you to shed the bad stuff and to keep it away from you for the long haul. Be super-honest with them as they hold you accountable, celebrate your successes and give you additional tips.

CONCLUSION

Now is the time for courage. Courage is action in the presence of fear. You can focus on the fear of what others might think about your new choices, or you can focus on your future that is filled with thriving relationships, doing the work you love, and accomplishing that bucket list of fulfilling experiences.

Be grateful that you have come to this season of your life when you say enough is enough with letting the wrong kind of things attach to your life to the extent it has limited your progress. Be grateful that you have the new resolve and some tools to pull off that old self, and to put on people and perspectives that will take you beyond what you previously thought impossible.

And the next time your dryer ends its cycle and alerts you it's done and buzzes, may it always remind you of your action plan that you formed while reading *The Static Cling Principle*.

ABOUT THE AUTHOR

Paul D. Casey has been a professional speaker for over twenty years and one of the leading authorities in leadership and personal growth. He has a master's degree in education, and has been a chief operating officer, educator, and administrator in several large non-profit organizations.

Currently, Paul contributes daily inspirational growth messages on local radio. He has inspired thousands of individuals and leaders through his seminars, his focused group retreats, and as a key note speaker. Through his company, Growing Forward Services, Paul has partnered with his clients to transform their lives.

Residing in Washington State, Paul and his wife Laura are being coached by their two children Austin and Cheyenne. For fun, he enjoys golfing, hiking, and biking.

Paul's personal mission statement is "To add value to others through equipping/encouraging words, servant-leader actions, and a contagious passion to honor God with his life." Faith, family, and growth are his top three values in life, and he is an insatiable life-long learner.

APPENDIX

Instructions: From this list of values, circle the ones that you wholeheartedly believe are important, leave the ones blank that you partially believe are important, and cross out the ones that are not important to you at all. Feel free to add other values that are not on this sample list.

After that, look at the circled values, and determine which ten are the most important to you.

Finally, rank your top five values—the ones that you must have in your relationships and workplace in order to stay true to who you are and what you believe. These are your DNA!

The Static Cling Principle

- ❑ achievement/success
- ❑ autonomy
- ❑ beauty
- ❑ challenge
- ❑ communication
- ❑ competence
- ❑ competition
- ❑ courage
- ❑ creativity
- ❑ curiosity
- ❑ decisiveness
- ❑ dependability
- ❑ discipline
- ❑ diversity
- ❑ effectiveness
- ❑ empathy
- ❑ equality
- ❑ family
- ❑ flexibility
- ❑ freedom
- ❑ friendship
- ❑ growth
- ❑ happiness
- ❑ harmony
- ❑ health
- ❑ honesty/integrity
- ❑ hope
- ❑ humor

- ❑ independence
- ❑ innovation
- ❑ intelligence
- ❑ love/affection
- ❑ loyalty
- ❑ open-mindedness
- ❑ patience
- ❑ power
- ❑ productivity
- ❑ prosperity/wealth
- ❑ quality
- ❑ recognition
- ❑ respect
- ❑ risk-taking
- ❑ security
- ❑ service
- ❑ simplicity
- ❑ spirituality/faith
- ❑ strength
- ❑ teamwork
- ❑ trust
- ❑ truth
- ❑ variety
- ❑ wisdom
- ❑ ________________
- ❑ ________________
- ❑ ________________
- ❑ ________________

CPSIA information can be obtained
at www.ICGtesting.com
Printed in the USA
FSOW01n1546160816
23761FS